Pat Marvenko Smith's Revelation artwork series has garnered accolades from many highly respected Christian teachers and evangelists who have used her art in their ministries and on their programs over the years.

"It has been my privilege to use the prophetic pictorial concepts of Pat Marvenko Smith for many years. Pat has a grasp of prophetic scripture that she reveals through her masterful works of art making the Book of Revelation graphic and alive." **John C. Hagee, Senior Pastor Cornerstone Church, San Antonio, Texas**

"These magnificent Revelation paintings by Pat Marvenko Smith faithfully illustrate the Bible text down to the last detail. They're dramatic, startling, and breathtakingly beautiful! " **Dr. Jack Van Impe, Jack Van Impe Ministries International**

"I consider Pat Marvenko Smith to be Christendom's foremost illustrator of the book of Revelation. Her illustrations are biblically accurate, visually inspiring, and glorifying to God. They are also adaptable to illustrating any prophetic viewpoint of the book." **Dr. David Reagan, Lamb & Lion Ministries**

"Art is frozen music. Pat Marvenko Smith has captured the music of heaven and frozen it on the canvas. Revelation Illustrated is stunning and inspired. Visions of heaven and time have never been more fascinating!" **Rod Hembree, Pastor Good Friends Fellowship and Executive producer of Quick Study TV**

"Pat Marvenko Smith's beautiful artwork has graced the pages of Prophecy in the News for many years. Her artistic talents have been shared willingly and our readers have been the fortunate recipients of her prophetic vision." **J.R. Church, Prophecy in the News**

"Pat Marvenko Smith provides a powerful visual reference for anyone who desires quality prints of end-time events. I have long found her artwork as a helpful tool to better communicate the words of biblical prophecy." **Dr. John Ankerberg, founder and president of The John Ankerberg Show**

"Pat Marvenko Smith's illustrations of the Book of Revelation are biblically accurate, artistically exceptional, and stunningly insightful." **Dr. Ed Hindson, Distinguished Professor at Liberty University and host of "The King is Coming" telecast**

"It has been my pleasure to incorporate Pat's illustrations into our ministry materials. She truly captures the essence of prophetic scripture and translates this into graphic presentations which speak to those who are fortunate enough to see it." **Dr. Morris Cerullo, President Morris Cerullo World Evangelism**

"We were thrilled to be able to use Pat Marvenko Smith's artwork in our film *Left Behind: Tribulation Force*. Her two pieces, "Four Horsemen" and "The Two Witnesses" lent a richness, texture and realism to our film which carried through many important scenes." **Paul Lalonde, Executive Producer**

Copyright © 2015 Pat Marvenko Smith.

All rights reserved. No part of this book may be used or reproduced by any means, graphic, electronic, or mechanical, including photocopying, recording, taping or by any information storage retrieval system without the written permission of the publisher except in the case of brief quotations embodied in critical articles and reviews.

WestBow Press books may be ordered through booksellers or by contacting:

WestBow Press
A Division of Thomas Nelson & Zondervan
1663 Liberty Drive
Bloomington, IN 47403
www.westbowpress.com
1 (866) 928-1240

All artwork in this book is created by Pat Marvenko Smith and is protected and registered with the Library of Congress, Washington D.C., USA, under United States international copyright number VAu 39-436, dated May 5, 1982, addendum October 5 1992, under the title of REVELATION ILLUSTRATED; a series of full color illustrations of Revelation, the last book of the Bible. No part of this artwork may be copied in any manner for any use, whatsoever without written permission from the artist.

Revelation Productions
1740 Ridgeview Drive
North Huntingdon, PA 15642
www.revelationillustrated.com

Because of the dynamic nature of the Internet, any web addresses or links contained in this book may have changed since publication and may no longer be valid. The views expressed in this work are solely those of the author and do not necessarily reflect the views of the publisher, and the publisher hereby disclaims any responsibility for them.

Any people depicted in stock imagery provided by Thinkstock are models, and such images are being used for illustrative purposes only. Certain stock imagery © Thinkstock.

ISBN: 978-1-4908-9134-7 (sc)
ISBN: 978-1-4908-9135-4 (e)

Print information available on the last page.

WestBow Press rev. date: 09/29/2015

Revelation Illustrated
An Artist's View of the Bible's Last Book

by

Pat Marvenko Smith

Acknowledgements

First, I thank the Lord for His guidance and inspiration through His word and His Holy Spirit.

I'm thankful for my loving parents Rose and John Marvenko for recognizing my giftedness at an early age and encouraging me throughout my life.

Thank you to my husband Joel D. Smith (J.D.) for his love, support, patience, and for using his business and computer skills to manage Revelation Productions and for typing and laying out this book.

Thank you to our sons Reuben and Ryan for their love, support and understanding through the years.

I am grateful to my dear sister Kathy Davis for using her literary and proofreading skills for this book.

Thank you to my sister Paula Zadroga for always having words of encouragement and for her prayers.

Thank you to the River Hill Church of Christ for your prayers and for always being so supportive.

Last but certainly not least, I thank a dear brother in Christ, Bill Hilliker for following God's leading and making the publishing of this book possible.

Pat Marvenko Smith
Revelation Productions
www.revelationillustrated.com

A MESSAGE FROM THE ARTIST

My Beginnings As An Artist, and the Most Important Job In My Career

For as far back as I can remember I have been an artist, first making crayon "murals" on the underside of my mom's kitchen table at a very early age (which she did not appreciate) and drawing on every blank scrap of paper that I could find as a kid. I owe much to my parents John and Rose Marvenko, who recognized my talent early on and lovingly supported and encouraged me. When I was only 5 years old they enrolled me in oil painting classes! From 6th grade all the way through high school they drove me to free art classes at the Carnegie Institute of Pittsburgh where I spent every Saturday morning, which was a sacrifice for everyone involved. But it was a great discipline for me artistically. I actually started making an income from my artistic talents right out of high school. On the merits of my art portfolio I was hired by the home office of the G.C. Murphy Company in McKeesport, Pennsylvania where I worked in the sales promotion and advertising departments doing merchandise and fashion illustration for their newspaper tabloid advertisements. During that time my evenings were spent attending Carnegie Institute of Technology in Pittsburgh for fine art, which is now Carnegie Mellon University. After marriage to my husband Joel in 1968 I continued to work, but after my twin sons were born in 1975, I started doing freelance artwork from home to be a stay at home mom. I did fashion illustration for department stores, and various types of commercial illustration work for several ad agencies in the Pittsburgh area. I also did freelance advertising artwork for the Thrift and Treasury Drug Store home office for 11 years. So I have been a commercial artist and illustrator for most of my adult life. Throughout my career I have done illustration jobs for large and small companies, ministries and publishers. But I am certain that no "assignment" in my career as an artist has ever been as important, or as humbling as this one.

The Story Behind How the Artwork in This Book Was Inspired

Though I was raised in a Christian home, accepted Jesus as my savior and was baptized in my teens, in my twenties I had slowly grown farther away from the Lord. In my early thirties, desiring a renewed personal relationship with Jesus, I rededicated my life to the Lord and this time I also dedicated my talents to Him. Up to this point, in my professional life I had only been doing commercial artwork that was used in the secular world such as fashion illustration and product illustration that were ultimately used in newspapers and magazines. They would be looked at and then thrown away. There came a point when I feel that I was being led to do something that would be here long after I was gone. Something that would benefit others and not be thrown out in tomorrow's garbage. I prayed that God would lead me to an art project that would glorify Him, but I really did not know how He could use an artist. About six months after that prayer I reluctantly accepted a request to teach a teen Sunday School class at our small church near Monongahela, Pennsylvania. I wanted to be obedient to the Lord, even if it was completely out of my comfort zone. When I asked the students what book of the Bible they would like to study next, they all requested the Book of Revelation! In the Spring of 1981 I began preparing to teach the this challenging book to that junior and senior high school Sunday school class. I was not at all confident as a teacher, especially of such a difficult book. But I remembered from the scriptures that God uses ordinary people with various backgrounds and talents to serve Him, and I knew that He would help me as I stepped out in faith. I asked Him to fill me anew with the Holy Spirit in order to do what He wanted me to do, and I was confident that He would give me exactly what I needed to teach this class. Little did I know that he would give me a gift that would ultimately go far beyond my own need.

As I began my preparation to teach Revelation, the Holy Spirit revealed three things to me. First, my eyes fell upon Revelation 1:3, which reads, *"Blessed is the one who reads the words of this prophecy, and blessed are those who hear it and take to heart what is written in it, because the time is near"*. What an encouragement to know that I would receive a blessing simply by reading this book and taking its words to heart! How much more of a blessing is it to be able to teach this message? Then as I fearfully pondered the enormity of the Book of Revelation and all of its mysteries, this second message came to my mind, "Don't be overwhelmed by the whole book, but take it one verse at a time, because that is how it was written!". The third epiphany would ultimately change my life forever. As I read Apostle John's vivid and detailed descriptions of the visions that were given to him by the Lord, I knew without a doubt that the best way to teach this book, was with visual illustrations of those visions.

I started to re-read the Book of Revelation, and my eyes fell upon the verse that I know the Lord wanted to impress upon my heart. I believe that it is the key to understanding this complex book of the Bible. It is Apostle John's proclamation, *"I was in the Spirit on the Lord's day…"*. My goodness! That was it! We can't have a chance of figuring any of it out if we don't have the Holy Spirit within us to guide us, just as John did as he received the message! I had already prayed for the Holy Spirit to guide me as I read and prepared to teach Revelation. I also asked Him to remove any preconceived ideas and fears and that He would open my eyes and my mind to what He wanted me to know or see. I also prayed that I would be able to teach this small group of students in the most effective way possible. As I read on, I was amazed at how visual Revelation was. Why hadn't I noticed this when I had read it in the past? This time while I was reading the first chapter, I could easily visualize the details in the vision of the glorified Christ that the apostle was describing! It was so clear to me! I thought that the Book of Revelation was an artist's dream and that surely there had been many artists that had already illustrated it. Figuring that there were already visual teaching materials available out there somewhere to help supplement my teaching, I searched the Christian bookstores, but I was told that no visual materials existed for teaching this final book of prophecy. I was totally shocked to hear this! I also searched the local library and the few visual representations I did find were not completely true to scripture, incomplete, very old, outdated in style, and only in black and white. I felt that none of them accurately represented the exciting and dramatic visions I saw as I read Revelation. I could "see" in my mind's eye these fantastic visions so clearly, and they were in vivid color, which is such an important symbolic detail to understanding the messages. It was at that point that I realized if I wanted to teach my class with visual aids, I would have to create them myself.

A Supernatural Power Surge of Creativity

I gathered several good books written by respected Christian experts on the Book of Revelation, and I began my preparation for teaching. First I would pray for guidance to teach Revelation effectively. Then I would read the scriptures and prepare my lesson considering various author's opinions on the meanings of the visions described in the Book of Revelation. After that, I would read the scripture again and again, asking for God's guidance to illustrate the visions that were described in His word. Some visions were immediately crystal clear and in exciting technicolor in my mind as soon as I read them, while others took much more time and even fasting for several days! The creating of one illustration during which I actually felt demonic forces opposing me was "War In Heaven; Michael Defeats the Dragon" from chapter 12. That one took over a month to do. Only after fasting and praying for 3 days was I able to finish that one. A few times I awoke in the middle of the night with the inspiration of how to do an illustration that I had been praying about. I would always clear my mind of any preconceived ideas, so it was just like the blank drawing board before me. I would ask for the Holy Spirit to fill the void. Eventually, the pictures took shape. First in my mind, I believe inspired by the Holy Spirit, and then on the illustration board in pencil and then eventually in full color. This may sound strange, but at times I would feel a supernatural power surge of creativity that would start at the top of my head, travel through my body and out the tip of my paintbrush!

The Revelation art series was actually done in two separate groups. The first group of 19 illustrations were done in 1981 through 1982 while I was teaching over a period of 9 months. The second group of 21 illustrations were done 10 years later in 1992, while I prepared to produce the "Revelation Illustrated" video. I needed more illustrations to complete the story on Revelation, filled in some of the visual gaps that I had not had time to do while teaching it the first time. That explains why there are two copyright dates on my Revelation art series. The artwork was done in opaque and transparent watercolors and also in airbrushed acrylics. In a few of the earlier illustrations I even used regular enamel paint from spray cans because I could not afford an airbrush and a compressor to achieve the look and effect that I had in my mind. If you take a look at "The Four Horsemen" please note that the background was done with matte "barbecue black" and reddish auto body primer! When funds are minimal you have to be extra creative! The illustration process was exciting but also tiring. I felt a real responsibility to my students to capture every detail of the scripture as accurately as I could because I knew that they would remember what they saw longer than what they heard or read.

There was one particular incident which made me realize without a doubt that God was guiding my creative endeavor. While at the library gathering some research materials, for some reason I felt led to check out some classical recordings. I knew almost nothing about classical music and really never cared much for it, but I thought that maybe I would just listen to some soothing music while doing my artwork. That evening I started to illustrate chapter four of Revelation, while at that same time I began listening to the musical works of George Frederick Handel. The music helped tremendously while I was illustrating the description of the vision in which Apostle John describes the "Emerald Throne Scene In Heaven". I'll never forget as I was painting the tiny faces of the singing angels in that glorious heavenly scene and suddenly realizing that the very words being sung at that moment, *"Worthy is the Lamb that was slain, to receive honor and glory and blessing..."*, were the very words I was illustrating! I broke down into tears of joy and amazement. I later came to learn that Handel was also led by the Lord to do his great "Messiah" and he used many of the scriptures from Revelation. There were many other little incidents that happened to me that made me realize again and again that the Lord was in control of what I was doing. The addition of these visual interpretations of the difficult to imagine visions in Revelation truly enhanced my students' ability to remember what they learned in my classes. After that class was over I felt led to do much more with the artwork the Lord had given me. Inspired by the artwork I had produced, our pastor Stan Ott suggested that I think of a way to share the Revelation artwork with the whole congregation. My husband Joel, my cousin Jim Julian and I decided to put together a slide presentation, set to classical music recordings, with Jim doing the narration of the scriptures. We would call the presentation **"Revelation Illustrated"**.

Spiritual Warfare Begins

It was the point when we decided to do something with this artwork that would allow it to be shared with many more people that I would begin to realize exactly why the book of Revelation had not been illustrated and put into print before. When we made the decision to put this art series into a form that would have the potential to reach many more people with the message of Revelation, the attacks began. I was working on a title page for our presentation that would serve as the beginning for our slide presentation. With the artwork unfinished on my drawing board, I left for a youth group activity at our church camp where I was to be a chaperone. The winter day was cold but sunny, and the roads were perfectly dry. I took a wrong turn, and just as I rounded a bend there was a huge patch of ice all the way across the road that threw my car into an uncontrollable spin and sent it crashing into the guard rail. I sat dazed and completely baffled because there had not been a bit of ice or snow anywhere! With my seat belt fastened, I did not seem to be injured except for a slight bump on my knee. I seemed fine ... until the next day when I tried to complete my unfinished artwork. My right hand, the one with which I draw, was the only part of me that was affected and it was almost paralyzed with excruciating pain! Was this merely a coincidence? Or was it Satan's attempt to stop me from finishing the Revelation artwork series? It did seem like that to me, since it temporarily prevented me from finishing the work that God had given me to do. After several months of therapy and much prayer, I was finally able to finish that illustration.

Upon completion of that first series of artwork, we had to photograph it all so that we could put together the slide presentation. At that point there came another frightening attack. My husband Joel, an amateur photographer had pretty good equipment with which to shoot the slides of my art. He purchased a new copystand equipped with high intensity copy lights. With a copystand, the artwork can be photographed lying flat, with the camera attached above and parallel to the art. Joel turned on the copy lights, placed the first illustration on the stand and leaned down to look into the camera. Suddenly fire and sparks shot out of the two lights, singeing his hair! Realizing this was strange for a new piece of equipment, he checked the wiring, but found that it was perfect. There was no physical reason why it should have malfunctioned. Again and again the same thing happened, but only when my Revelation artwork was laid on the copy stand. Finally, I realized this was being caused by something supernatural, and it certainly was not from God! After much prayer, we were finally able to shoot the first roll of film without the pyrotechnics. On the same roll of film, Joel had also shot photos of some of my other artwork that did not deal with Revelation. When we got the slides back, all the shots of the Revelation artwork turned out completely black! The others were just fine. This happened several times. After more intense prayer, we finally did get the artwork onto slides. By the way, that copy stand has worked perfectly ever since that incident.

Shortly thereafter, my twin sons who were age 6 at that time became gravely ill with fevers that reached $105^{\circ}F$. They were both hospitalized within weeks of each other, both diagnosed with double pneumonia. Praise God, they did recover and have been fine ever since. Not long after that, my husband's job of 19 years with U.S. Steel was terminated. Within a very short period of time every member of our family had been attacked in some way. I truly believe these were Satan's attempts to discourage us and stop us from going forward with a project that would graphically depict his final and fiery destruction. In "Revelation Illustrated" people would <u>see</u> God's word come to life. They could see and hear the promises that Satan does not want them to know about; that Satan is a loser and Jesus Christ is the victor, and in Him we too are victorious! At the time we did not realize that "Revelation Illustrated" would touch thousands and then ultimately hundreds of thousands of lives all over the world. The slide program we finally put together was so enthusiastically received that we got numerous requests to show it at churches of all denominations. Thus began a traveling ministry that continued for ten years to over 600 church congregations, conventions and Bible study groups. We traveled together in our little equipment-packed van with our two young sons for a period of 10 years. From 1982 to 1992 we traveled to 8 states and Canadian provinces. Many people came to the Lord, and many got excited about studying the only book of the Bible they had previously feared. We had won the first round, and just as in past history Satan's attempts could not stop God's word.

When He Leads, He Will Provide

Through the ten years of showing that slide presentation, my husband was never able to regain a steady and stable job situation, but this only served to bring us closer to the Lord and to each other. There came a point around 1984 when Joel's unemployment checks had run out and our savings were depleted. It was at that point the Lord showed us that we needed to take a huge step in faith and put all the artwork into visual teaching materials to help other teachers. Everywhere we traveled to show our Revelation program people constantly asked if we had prints they could buy so they could teach with them or use them as a witnessing tool. Then I was asked to be a guest and show my art on a few different a Christian television talk shows. One of those shows in Canada was called "100 Huntley Street", which was a new and great experience. We returned home after that show to get about 700 letters from viewers also asking for copies of the art. It's an amazing feeling when you are absolutely certain that God is truly speaking to your heart to do something huge and expensive like that. Even when all common sense would tell you it's crazy to spend money you do not have, when He is leading you, it feels like the right thing to be doing. You have a peace about it, knowing that when He leads, He will provide. We put our trust completely in our Lord Jesus and took great steps in faith to produce the full color print sets and also slides (this was before Powerpoint) in an effort to provide a source of visual teaching materials that were previously not available. The Lord provided miraculously for us to pay off our huge production costs as hundreds of orders came in. One of my favorite Bible verses from Proverbs 3:5-6 described our situation so perfectly. *"Trust in the Lord with all your heart and lean not on your own understanding; in all your ways acknowledge Him and He will direct your paths."*

Amazing "Miracles" Lead to the Making of the Revelation Illustrated Video

After ten years of traveling with the multimedia slide presentation, we were led by many requests and by the Holy Spirit, to produce a video based on the slide program. With the video, many more people could experience "Revelation Illustrated" and much more could be done with computer generated special effects to bring the word of God to life. Years before the video was even an idea in my mind, the Lord had a plan. Now in retrospect I can see it, He had placed many talented Christian people in my path whom I would later call upon to help me in all phases of the audio and video production. This next step in faith brought about many amazing "miracles" for us. That's what I call them, because I recognized God's hand in so many things that happened.

We really had no money with which to produce a video. So, I prayed and laid my whole project before the throne of God. I told Him that I would step out in faith and produce that video and I would depend solely on Him to provide. That same day I started making calls to obtain estimates and make appointments for the music, recording and videotaping. It would be very expensive, but I started to make the arrangements anyway. One week later I received a call from John Lang, who was at that time executive director at Jack Van Impe Ministries. Someone there had sent for my brochure from an ad I had run in Charisma Magazine. They were making me an unbelievable offer to use all of my artwork from the Revelation Illustrated series in a teaching video called Revelation Revealed. Their use of my art would ultimately allow me to pay for almost half of my video project! When I met with Dr. Van Impe and Mr. Lang, they told me that they had made the decision to use my artwork in a meeting the week before they called me. That meeting had taken place on the very day I had prayed that prayer of faith, putting God in complete control of the video project! Indeed He <u>was</u> in control.

I remember the day of my appointment to meet with the manager of one of the biggest recording studios in Pittsburgh for an estimate to have the Revelation Illustrated video sound track done. Even though I had prayed about this and even fasted for three days before, I felt intimidated as I walked into the huge beautifully decorated, state of the art audio recording studio. Imagine my surprise to find that the manager, Gregg was someone I had met years before. He had once worked at another smaller studio and had come to my little office to contract the use one of my illustrations for an album cover for a local Christian musical group. I knew that Gregg was a Christian, but was really pleased to discover that most of those who worked for him were also Christians. I took that as a sign that this studio was the one I should use. Our first meeting went far beyond my expectations as Gregg informed me that we could actually hire part of a world renowned orchestra to do the classical sound track, the Pittsburgh Symphony Orchestra! He said that because of the size of his studio, the symphony often recorded various projects there. My cousin Jim Julian, a professional singer and voice teacher, suggested we use the Bach Choir of Pittsburgh and through Jim we were able to hire them to do the choral parts. Jim would also narrate on the video as the voice of John, as he had done years earlier for our slide presentation. My acquaintance in past years with Tom Green, a multiple Billboard award winning Christian TV producer, was also in God's plan and I was blessed and honored to be able to have Tom work as producer of our video. Tom, in turn hired a staff of technicians from Cornerstone Christian Television near Pittsburgh who would direct and edit with artistic passion, their love for the Lord so apparent in their lives and in their work.

Our ten years of showing the multi media slide program had yielded many names and addresses of those who wanted to be informed when the video based on that program was made. After just one mailing, we received hundreds of pre-orders from so many wonderful spirit-led, faithful people for a video that did not yet exist, which enabled us to pay for another part of the huge production costs that would follow. We eventually re-mortgaged our small home to cover the rest of the production cost.

A Bolt of Lightning Hits

With the beginning of production on the video came new attacks in Satan's attempt to stop it. It was a beautiful August day when we were scheduled to begin the recording of the sound track. It had taken months to gather all the classical pieces and have them arranged for our project. Everyone was keyed up for the big recording day. An hour and a half before all the musicians and singers were scheduled to arrive at the studio, I got a desperate call from Gregg the manager of the studio. There was no electrical power! The studio was in total darkness and we would not be able to record. He said there had just been a sudden thunderstorm in Pittsburgh and then he noted, it was really strange, because it had not affected all of Pittsburgh, but just the area of the studio. A bolt of lightning had struck a transformer on their block! The utility workers told Gregg that it would take hours to fix. Immediately after hanging up the phone, I placed a call to our church's prayer chain and asked them to pray that Satan would be bound and not be able to interfere. Once again as we were starting a new project he was trying his evil best to stop it before it began! From my previous experiences I knew that prayer was the only answer and there is definitely strength in numbers! Within 30 minutes the station manager called me back, exclaiming that the power was back on. **Indeed it was!** The sound track was recorded successfully with only a few minor disruptions.

That Old Red Dragon Thrown Into the Lake of Fire

As we began the videotaping and editing phase of the video project, Satan's attacks became more desperate and personal as he began to attack me physically. My health had always been great. No problems at all. Then during the two months it took to tape and edit the artwork, I was struck with three different health problems that resulted in surgeries and other hospital procedures. The ulcerative colitis was the worst and most painful problem, and at times I really thought I was dying. Doctors told me there was no cure. I was down, but not defeated. I never missed a video editing session, and I was determined not to complain because to do so would be to acknowledge a victory for the evil one. I was even more determined to overcome Satan by completing this video project successfully. Tom, my video producer was also struck, and he became very ill at the same time with serious heart problems. Many times during the long hours of editing, he would have to go to his office to lie down. His problem subsided after the production was over. The ulcerative colitis that had made me so ill, eventually went into complete remission, and I am now symptom-free. I'll never forget the absolute delight that I felt as we all watched for the first time the scene in the video where Satan, that old red dragon is thrown into the lake of fire that burns forever! As the scene in the video shows the flames licking at his tail and slowly enveloping him, his desperate screams and howls of final defeat are loudly heard. A loud cheer went up in the video editing suite of the studio that day, from all of us who were watching. Oh, how I look forward to the day when that happens in reality. I know a cheer will resound throughout all of heaven as all the saints and martyrs of all ages witness that event.

Faith Is Indeed the Victory

If I had known before I illustrated the Book of Revelation, of the frightening events that would follow, perhaps I would not have used my artistic talents in such a way. But oh, how glad I am that I was obedient to my Lord Jesus. Through it all I have grown so much stronger in my walk with Him. I have learned the real live meaning of a scripture that I repeated over and over throughout those tough times, *"Greater is He that is in you, than he that is in the world"* from 1st John 4:4. But most importantly, I feel that I have faithfully used my talents in the way the Lord has led me. He has allowed me to accomplish so much more than I ever dreamed, and has been my strength through it all. We rarely see large profits at year's end, but the consistent calls, emails and enthusiastic words of encouragement from our wonderful customers remind me that it has all been worth it. The Lord is truly using *Revelation Illustrated* in a mighty way for his Kingdom. The art has been seen by people in almost every country in the world, via the Internet as evidenced by our website tracker. Since we started to produce the visual materials from this artwork we have provided tens of thousands of prints, slides and overhead transparencies, videos, DVDs and digital image CDs to Bible teachers and laypeople alike, for a clearer understanding of this most marvelous book of God's promises. And now God has graciously provided us with the means to publish this artwork in book form also. As a teaching aid this series of artwork is being sought after by teachers and pastors of all Christian denominations. As a witnessing tool it has inspired many people to give their lives to the Lord. That is the power of God's word, especially in graphic form. The effect of His word within us can be doubled when it is seen, as well as heard. The Lord Jesus knew this when He revealed the message to Apostle John and He knew it when He inspired me to create this artwork from that message. The illustrated word of God can transcend language barriers and even minister to the illiterate. No wonder Satan had tried so hard to stop **"Revelation Illustrated"** from being produced! I praise God for this victory. He is so awesome!

God had a great and beautiful plan from the moment He led me to teach that Sunday school class. I am so glad that I obeyed Him in faith and accepted that challenge. And through the years I'm so glad I stood firm in my belief that this is what I have been "called" to do. To this day, I am told by some of the greatest teachers and experts on Revelation, that my artwork is the most complete and accurate that is available on the book! I'm sure it is because it was inspired by "The Author". My life has been totally changed by the events that resulted and it thrills my heart to know that the lives of hundreds of thousands of others around the world have also been touched and even changed by **"Revelation Illustrated"** !

Why Is the Book of Revelation So Important Now?

The Book of Revelation is the last book in the New Testament and it is one of the Bible's most visual books in the Bible. The messages of praise, warning, and hope were given to the Apostle John by the victorious risen Christ in the form of fantastic visions. John faithfully recorded those important messages in intricate detail. Every color, every number, every object in every vision has meaning and has been written there for us to read and ponder and heed and share.

The Revelation of John, or the Apocalypse as it is sometimes called is the only book of prophecy in the New Testament, and the only book of Biblical prophecy yet to be completely fulfilled. And we can certainly be assured that it will. Why can we be so sure of this? Because the Old Testament contains over 300 prophetic messages foretelling the first coming of Jesus Christ to this earth, and every last one of them came true, down to very detail. So by this we can know without a doubt that the prophetic message of Christ's second coming in Revelation will also come true.

The message in the Book of Revelation was given to the Apostle John while he was in exile on the Isle of Patmos during the reign of Roman emperor Domitian around 96 AD. The Christians at that time in history were under terrible persecution by the Roman Empire and this message was needed to give them guidance and hope. That message is for us now as it was then. But why is the Book of Revelation so important now? The Book of Revelation, declares the absolute Lordship of Jesus Christ and tells us of His glorious return. No one knows the exact time or day when Jesus will return, but it is important that we all be ready to meet Him at any time. Revelation also very clearly depicts the rewards of his followers as well as the punishment of those who reject Him. God's word is timeless, and that same message still gives Christians today the wonderful promise that He is in control no matter what happens. And those who remain faithful will dwell with Him forever in eternity in the new heavens and the new earth. **What a wonderful promise!**

But the Book of Revelation frightens me .... I just don't understand it ...

Sadly, many Christians, totally avoid Revelation. Many pastors won't even preach on it. And I believe that this is exactly what Satan wants! Of all the books in the Bible, none tells us so specifically or so graphically of what Satan's final fiery end will be. He is a loser and he wants to stop as many people as he can from finding out that fact. So he puts excuses and fears in our minds. There are basically two reasons people give for avoiding the Book of Revelation, "it frightens me", and "I can't understand it". If you have ever made either of those excuses, then I first of all must commend you for picking up this book! After seeing the message of Revelation in pictures, I believe you will view Revelation in a totally new light. You will gain a clearer view of the message of this wonderful book from God's word when you actually see it pictured.

To those who say they don't understand it, I must tell you that Bible scholars and teachers who have devoted much of their lives to studying Revelation may admit that even they do not understand all of the Book of Revelation and may not until Jesus returns. However, it is part of God's word for you. It was given to Apostle John while he was "in the Spirit", and that is the key to helping you to understand the Book of Revelation. The Holy Spirit will help you to understand exactly what the Lord wants you to know at that particular moment in your life. Within Revelation Jesus has given a universal message as well as a personal message for each one of us. Just like the rest of the Bible, God's word is timeless and God's word is for everyone. He has a message in there for you. Ask Him to help you find it.

If the Book of Revelation frightens you, please keep in mind that its message was originally given to comfort and to give hope and encouragement to Christians under great persecution. It assures us that those who do the persecuting and those who reject the Lord are the ones who will be will dealt with severely, for eternity. But God's children will be saved. Revelation tells of terrible destructive plagues sent by God to the earth. But remember all the past scriptures in the Bible that prove that our God is a God of compassion for His people and He always provides a way of escape. Remember the time in scripture where God sent the great flood to destroy the earth, but He made a way for those who were faithful to escape that flood. Noah and his family were the only ones, but they were kept from harm because of their obedience to God. Another great example of God's protection of those who are His is told in the story of the of the Israelites escape from Egyptian captivity. God sent the horrible plagues including the death angel that killed all of the first born in Egypt. But He spared His people, the Israelites. When they obediently applied the blood of a sacrificed lamb onto their doorposts, the death angel passed by their homes and did not destroy the first born living there. This is a wonderful prophetic symbol of Christ's sacrifice, the shedding of His blood for the atonement of our sins, thus saving us and making us His own. And we can be assured that He will protect His own. But as Noah and his family had to obey God and build the ark, and as the Israelites were told to paint the blood of the sacrificed lamb on their doorposts, we too must be obedient. We must accept Jesus, the Lamb of God into our hearts as our Lord and Savior. When we do, it's as if that blood is applied to our hearts and we are saved as the Israelites were. Our name is then written in the Lamb's Book of Life assuring that we will spend eternity in heaven!

Why Was Revelation Given In the Form of Visions?

I believe that the Lord Jesus Christ who gave us this message is the same Creator who made our brains with a right and a left side. And He knows how our minds most effectively process and retain information. He knows that we retain so much more when we can audibly receive a message while receiving that message visually as well. The right side of the brain is responsible for visualization. The left side is responsible for processing the information. When both sides of the brain are involved, the brain processes the information more efficiently for a more lasting impression. In addition the person is better prepared to use and apply their new knowledge. Jesus was giving a very important message to Apostle John, and John would need to later write it down in order to send it to the seven churches in the province of Asia. I believe that God knew that John would be sure to remember every detail if he were to hear the message and also see it at the same time in the form of visions. And that is how we can most effectively remember the message, too! I believe that this is why the Lord also inspired me to illustrate the visions described in Revelation. I also believe that He provided the means for me to do this book, the Revelation Illustrated video before it, and the prints before that so that this artwork can go on continuing to bring the message of Revelation in a more memorable way until Jesus returns. As people have viewed my artwork along with the scripture, they have told me that they have a much clearer understanding of the message God has for them in the Book of Revelation. To God be the glory!

In the pages that follow, you will view my whole Revelation artwork series with the entire scripture text from the Book of Revelation, taken from the King James Version. I have also chosen to add "The Rapture" illustration at the very end of this book, which was taken from 1st Thessalonians 4:16-18 and Matthew 24:40, which shows the return of Jesus for His bride, the church. The purpose of this book is to serve as a companion supplement to any study on the Book of Revelation that you choose to use, regardless of doctrinal or millennial viewpoint. That's because it is simply the word of God in pictures. There are countless books already written which give teachings and opinions concerning the message in the Book of Revelation. But this may be one of the very few that actually present the message of Revelation in the way that the prophetic message was originally presented, **visually!** Be blessed as you read the scriptures from the Book of Revelation, and at the same time view it through the eyes of an artist.

**Blessed is he that readeth, and they that
hear the words of this prophecy,
and keep those things which are written therein;
for the time is near.**

Revelation 1:3

Apostle John On the Isle of Patmos (Rev 1:9-11)

The Book of Revelation

Chapter 1

The Revelation of Jesus Christ, which God gave unto him, to show unto his servants things which must shortly come to pass; and he sent and signified it by his angel unto his servant John: ² Who bare record of the word of God, and of the testimony of Jesus Christ, and of all things that he saw. ³ Blessed is he that reads, and they that hear the words of this prophecy, and keep those things which are written therein: for the time is at hand. ⁴ John, to the seven churches which are in Asia: Grace be unto you, and peace, from him which is, and which was, and which is to come; and from the seven Spirits which are before his throne; ⁵ And from Jesus Christ, who is the faithful witness, and the first begotten of the dead, and the prince of the kings of the earth. Unto him that loved us, and washed us from our sins in his own blood,

⁶ And hath made us kings and priests unto God and his Father; to him be glory and dominion for ever and ever. Amen. ⁷ Behold, he cometh with clouds; and every eye shall see him, and they also which pierced him: and all kindreds of the earth shall wail because of him. Even so, Amen.

⁸ I am Alpha and Omega, the beginning and the ending, says the Lord, which is, and which was, and which is to come, the Almighty.

⁹ I John, who also am your brother, and companion in tribulation, and in the kingdom and patience of Jesus Christ, was in the isle that is called Patmos, for the word of God, and for the testimony of Jesus Christ. ¹⁰ I was in the Spirit on the Lord's day, and heard behind me a great voice, as of a trumpet, ¹¹ Saying, I am Alpha and Omega, the first and the last: and, What you see, write in a book, and send it unto the seven churches which are in Asia; unto Ephesus, and unto Smyrna, and unto Pergamos, and unto Thyatira, and unto Sardis, and unto Philadelphia, and unto Laodicea.

¹² And I turned to see the voice that spoke with me. And being turned, I saw seven golden candlesticks; ¹³ And in the midst of the seven candlesticks one like unto the Son of man, clothed with a garment down to the foot, and girt about the chest with a golden girdle. ¹⁴ His head and his hairs were white like wool, as white as snow; and his eyes were as a flame of fire; ¹⁵ And his feet like unto fine brass, as if they burned in a furnace; and his voice as the sound of many waters. ¹⁶ And he had in his right hand seven stars: and out of his mouth went a sharp two-edged sword: and his countenance was as the sun shineth in his strength.

¹⁷ And when I saw him, I fell at his feet as dead. And he laid his right hand upon me, saying unto me, Fear not; I am the first and the last:. ¹⁸ I am he that lived, and was dead; and, behold, I am alive for evermore, Amen; and have the keys of hell and of death. ¹⁹ Write the things which you have seen, and the things which are, and the things which shall be hereafter; ²⁰ The mystery of the seven stars which you saw in my right hand, and the seven golden candlesticks. The seven stars are the angels of the seven churches: and the seven candlesticks which you saw are the seven churches.

Chapter 2

Unto the angel of the church of Ephesus write; These things says he that holds the seven stars in his right hand, who walks in the midst of the seven golden candlesticks; ² I know thy works, and thy labor, and thy patience, and how you canst not bear them which are evil: and you have tried them which say they are apostles, and are not, and have found them liars: ³ And have borne, and have patience, and for my name's sake have labored, and have not fainted.

⁴ Nevertheless I have somewhat against thee, because you have left thy first love. ⁵ Remember therefore from whence you art fallen, and repent, and do the first works; or else I will come unto thee quickly, and will remove thy candlestick out of his place, except you repent. ⁶ But this you have, that you hate the deeds of the Nicolaitanes, which I also hate.

⁷ He that hath an ear, let him hear what the Spirit says unto the churches; To him that overcomes will I give to eat of the tree of life,

"And I turned to see the voice that spoke with me ..." (Rev 1:12)

Christ Amidst the Lampstands (Rev 1:12-20)

which is in the midst of the paradise of God.

⁸ And unto the angel of the church in Smyrna write; These things say the first and the last, which was dead, and is alive; ⁹ I know thy works, and tribulation, and poverty, (but you art rich) and I know the blasphemy of them which say they are Jews, and are not, but are the synagogue of Satan. ¹⁰ Fear none of those things which you shalt suffer: behold, the devil shall cast some of you into prison, that ye may be tried; and ye shall have tribulation ten days: be you faithful unto death, and I will give thee a crown of life.

¹¹ He that hath an ear, let him hear what the Spirit says unto the churches; He that overcomes shall not be hurt of the second death.

¹² And to the angel of the church in Pergamos write; These things says he which hath the sharp sword with two edges; ¹³ I know thy works, and where you dwell, even where Satan's seat is: and you hold fast my name, and have not denied my faith, even in those days wherein Antipas was my faithful martyr, who was slain among you, where Satan dwells. ¹⁴ But I have a few things against thee, because you have there them that hold the doctrine of Balaam, who taught Balac to cast a stumbling block before the children of Israel, to eat things sacrificed unto idols, and to commit fornication. ¹⁵ So have you also them that hold the doctrine of the Nicolaitanes, which thing I hate. ¹⁶ Repent; or else I will come unto thee quickly, and will fight against them with the sword of my mouth. ¹⁷ He that hath an ear, let him hear what the Spirit says unto the churches; To him that overcomes will I give to eat of the hidden manna, and will give him a white stone, and in the stone a new name written, which no man knows saving he that receives it.

¹⁸ And unto the angel of the church in Thyatira write; These things says the Son of God, who hath his eyes like unto a flame of fire, and his feet are like fine brass; ¹⁹ I know thy works, and charity, and service, and faith, and thy patience, and thy works; and the last to be more than the first.

²⁰ Notwithstanding I have a few things against thee, because you sufferest that woman Jezebel, which calls herself a prophetess, to teach and to seduce my servants to commit fornication, and to eat things sacrificed unto idols. ²¹ And I gave her space to repent of her fornication; and she repented not. ²² Behold, I will cast her into a bed, and them that commit adultery with her into great tribulation, except they repent of their deeds. ²³ And I will kill her children with death; and all the churches shall know that I am he who searches the reins and hearts: and I will give unto every one of you according to your works. ²⁴ But unto you I say, and unto the rest in Thyatira, as many as have not this doctrine, and which have not known the depths of Satan, as they speak; I will put upon you none other burden. ²⁵ But that which ye have already hold fast till I come. ²⁶ And he that overcomes, and keeps my works unto the end, to him will I give power over the nations:

²⁷ And he shall rule them with a rod of iron; as the vessels of a potter shall they be broken to shivers: even as I received of my Father. ²⁸ And I will give him the morning star. ²⁹ He that hath an ear, let him hear what the Spirit says unto the churches.

Chapter 3

And unto the angel of the church in Sardis write; These things says he that hath the seven Spirits of God, and the seven stars; I know thy works, that you have a name that you livest, and art dead. ² Be watchful, and strengthen the things which remain, that are ready to die: for I have not found thy works perfect before God. ³ Remember therefore how you have received and heard, and hold fast, and repent. If therefore you shalt not watch, I will come on thee as a thief, and you shalt not know what hour I will come upon thee.

⁴ You have a few names even in Sardis which have not defiled their garments; and they shall walk with me in white: for they are worthy. ⁵ He that overcomes, the same shall be clothed in white raiment; and I will not blot out his name out of the book of life, but I will confess his name before my Father, and before his angels. ⁶ He that hath an ear, let him hear what the Spirit says unto the churches.

⁷ And to the angel of the church in Philadelphia write; These things say he that is holy, he that is true, he that hath the key of David, he that opens, and no man shuts; and shuts, and no man opens; ⁸ I know thy works: behold, I have set before thee an open door, and no man can shut it: for you have a little strength, and have kept my word, and have not denied my name. ⁹ Behold, I will make them of the synagogue of Satan, which say they are Jews, and are not, but do lie; behold, I will make them to come and worship before thy feet, and to know that I have loved thee. ¹⁰ Because you have kept the word of my patience, I also will keep thee from the hour of temptation, which shall come upon all the world, to try them that dwell upon the earth.

[11] Behold, I come quickly: hold that fast which you have, that no man take thy crown. [12] Him that overcomes will I make a pillar in the temple of my God, and he shall go no more out: and I will write upon him the name of my God, and the name of the city of my God, which is new Jerusalem, which comes down out of heaven from my God: and I will write upon him my new name. [13] He that hath an ear, let him hear what the Spirit says unto the churches.

[14] And unto the angel of the church of the Laodiceans write; These things saith the Amen, the faithful and true witness, the beginning of the creation of God; [15] I know thy works, that you art neither cold nor hot: I would you wert cold or hot. [16] So then because you art lukewarm, and neither cold nor hot, I will spue thee out of my mouth.

[17] Because you say, I am rich, and increased with goods, and have need of nothing; and know not that you art wretched, and miserable, and poor, and blind, and naked: [18] I counsel thee to buy of me gold tried in the fire, that you may be rich; and white raiment, that you may be clothed, and that the shame of thy nakedness do not appear; and anoint your eyes with eyesalve, that you may see.

[19] As many as I love, I rebuke and chasten: be zealous therefore, and repent. [20] Behold, I stand at the door, and knock: if any man hear my voice, and open the door, I will come in to him, and will sup with him, and he with me.

[21] To him that overcomes will I grant to sit with me in my throne, even as I also overcame, and am set down with my Father in his throne. [22] He that hath an ear, let him hear what the Spirit says unto the churches.

Map of the Seven Churches of Asia and the Isle of Patmos

The Open Door in Heaven (Rev 4:1)

Chapter 4

After this I looked, and, behold, a door was opened in heaven: and the first voice which I heard was as it were of a trumpet talking with me; which said, Come up hither, and I will show thee things which must be hereafter. ² And immediately I was in the spirit: and, behold, a throne was set in heaven, and one sat on the throne. ³ And he that sat was to look upon like a jasper and a sardine stone: and there was a rainbow round about the throne, in sight like unto an emerald. ⁴ And round about the throne were four and twenty seats: and upon the seats I saw four and twenty elders sitting, clothed in white raiment; and they had on their heads crowns of gold. ⁵ And out of the throne proceeded lightning and thunder and voices: and there were seven lamps of fire burning before the throne, which are the seven Spirits of God. ⁶ And before the throne there was a sea of glass like unto crystal: and in the midst of the throne, and round about the throne, were four beasts full of eyes before and behind.

The Emerald Throne Scene in Heaven (Rev 4:2-11)

Casting Crowns Before the Throne (Rev 4:9-11)

⁷ And the first beast was like a lion, and the second beast like a calf, and the third beast had a face as a man, and the fourth beast was like a flying eagle. ⁸ And the four beasts had each of them six wings about him; and they were full of eyes within: and they rest not day and night, saying, Holy, holy, holy, LORD God Almighty, which was, and is, and is to come. ⁹ And when those beasts give glory and honor and thanks to him that sat on the throne, who lives for ever and ever, ¹⁰ The four and twenty elders fall down before him that sat on the throne, and worship him that lives for ever and ever, and cast their crowns before the throne, saying, ¹¹ You art worthy, O Lord, to receive glory and honor and power: for you have created all things, and for thy pleasure they are and were created.

The Strong Angel Proclaiming in a Loud Voice, "Who is worthy ..." (Rev 5:2)

Chapter 5

And I saw in the right hand of him that sat on the throne a book written within and on the backside, sealed with seven seals. ²And I saw a strong angel proclaiming with a loud voice, Who is worthy to open the book, and to loose the seals thereof? ³And no man in heaven, nor in earth, neither under the earth, was able to open the book, neither to look thereon. ⁴And I wept much, because no man was found worthy to open and to read the book, neither to look thereon. ⁵And one of the elders says unto me, Weep not: behold, the Lion of the tribe of Judah, the Root of David, hath prevailed to open the book, and to loose the seven seals thereof.

⁶And I beheld, and, lo, in the midst of the throne and of the four beasts, and in the midst of the elders, stood a Lamb as it had been slain, having seven horns and seven eyes, which are the seven Spirits of God sent forth into all the earth. ⁷And he came and took the

The Opening of the Sealed Scroll (Rev 5:5-14)

book out of the right hand of him that sat upon the throne. ⁸ And when he had taken the book, the four beasts and four and twenty elders fell down before the Lamb, having every one of them harps, and golden vials full of odors, which are the prayers of saints.

⁹ And they sung a new song, saying, Thou art worthy to take the book, and to open the seals thereof: for you were slain, and have redeemed us to God by thy blood out of every kindred, and tongue, and people, and nation;

¹⁰ And have made us unto our God kings and priests: and we shall reign on the earth. ¹¹And I beheld, and I heard the voice of many angels round about the throne and the beasts and the elders: and the number of them was ten thousand times ten thousand, and thousands of thousands; ¹² Saying with a loud voice, Worthy is the Lamb that was slain to receive power, and riches, and wisdom, and strength, and honor, and glory, and blessing.

¹³ And every creature which is in heaven, and on the earth, and under the earth, and such as are in the sea, and all that are in them, heard I saying, Blessing, and honor, and glory, and power, be unto him that sits upon the throne, and unto the Lamb for ever and ever. ¹⁴ And the four beasts said, Amen. And the four and twenty elders fell down and worshipped him that lives for ever and ever.

Chapter 6

And I saw when the Lamb opened one of the seals, and I heard, as it were the noise of thunder, one of the four beasts saying, Come and see. ² And I saw, and behold a white horse: and he that sat on him had a bow; and a crown was given unto him: and he went forth conquering, and to conquer.

The First Four Seals; Four Horsemen (Rev 6:1-8)

³ And when he had opened the second seal, I heard the second beast say, Come and see. ⁴ And there went out another horse that was red: and power was given to him that sat thereon to take peace from the earth, and that they should kill one another: and there was given unto him a great sword.

⁵ And when he had opened the third seal, I heard the third beast say, Come and see. And I beheld, and lo a black horse; and he that sat on him had a pair of balances in his hand. ⁶ And I heard a voice in the midst of the four beasts say, A measure of wheat for a penny, and three measures of barley for a penny; and see you hurt not the oil and the wine.

⁷ And when he had opened the fourth seal, I heard the voice of the fourth beast say, Come and see. ⁸ And I looked, and behold a pale horse: and his name that sat on him was Death, and Hell followed with him. And power was given unto them over the fourth part of the earth, to kill with sword, and with hunger, and with death, and with the beasts of the earth.

⁹ And when he had opened the fifth seal, I saw under the altar the souls of them that were slain for the word of God, and for the testimony which they held: ¹⁰ And they cried with a loud voice, saying, How long, O Lord, holy and true, dost you not judge and avenge our blood on them that dwell on the earth? ¹¹ And white robes were given unto every one of them; and it was said unto them, that they should rest yet for a little season, until their fellow servants also and their brethren, that should be killed as they were, should be fulfilled.

The Fifth Seal, Souls of the Martyrs (Rev 6:9-11)

The Sixth Seal; Destruction in Nature (Rev 6:12-17)

¹² And I beheld when he had opened the sixth seal, and, lo, there was a great earthquake; and the sun became black as sackcloth of hair, and the moon became as blood; ¹³ And the stars of heaven fell unto the earth, even as a fig tree casteth her untimely figs, when she is shaken of a mighty wind.

¹⁴ And the heaven departed as a scroll when it is rolled together; and every mountain and island were moved out of their places.

¹⁵ And the kings of the earth, and the great men, and the rich men, and the chief captains, and the mighty men, and every bondman, and every free man, hid themselves in the dens and in the rocks of the mountains; ¹⁶ And said to the mountains and rocks, Fall on us, and hide us from the face of him that sits on the throne, and from the wrath of the Lamb: ¹⁷ For the great day of his wrath is come; and who shall be able to stand?

Chapter 7

And after these things I saw four angels standing on the four corners of the earth, holding the four winds of the earth, that the wind should not blow on the earth, nor on the sea, nor on any tree. ² And I saw another angel ascending from the east, having the seal of the living God: and he cried with a loud voice to the four angels, to whom it was given to hurt the earth and the sea, ³ Saying, Hurt not the earth, neither the sea, nor the trees, till we have sealed the servants of our God in their foreheads. ⁴ And I heard the number of them which were sealed: and there were sealed an hundred and forty and four thousand of all the tribes of the children of Israel.

⁵ Of the tribe of Judah were sealed twelve thousand. Of the tribe of Reuben were sealed twelve thousand. Of the tribe of Gad were sealed twelve thousand. ⁶ Of the tribe of Aser were sealed twelve thousand. Of the tribe of Nephthalim were sealed twelve thousand. Of the tribe of Manasses were sealed twelve thousand. ⁷ Of the tribe of Simeon were sealed twelve thousand. Of the tribe of Levi were sealed twelve thousand. Of the tribe of Issachar were sealed twelve thousand. ⁸ Of the tribe of Zabulon were sealed twelve thousand. Of the tribe of Joseph were sealed twelve thousand. Of the tribe of Benjamin were sealed twelve thousand.

Receiving the Seal of God (Rev 7:2-8)

The 144,000 Sealed and the Multitude in White Robes (Rev 7:3-10)

⁹ After this I beheld, and, lo, a great multitude, which no man could number, of all nations, and kindreds, and people, and tongues, stood before the throne, and before the Lamb, clothed with white robes, and palms in their hands; ¹⁰ And cried with a loud voice, saying, Salvation to our God which sits upon the throne, and unto the Lamb.

¹¹ And all the angels stood round about the throne, and about the elders and the four beasts, and fell before the throne on their faces, and worshipped God, ¹² Saying, Amen: Blessing, and glory, and wisdom, and thanksgiving, and honor, and power, and might, be unto our God for ever and ever. Amen.

¹³ And one of the elders answered, saying unto me, What are these which are arrayed in white robes? From where have they come?

¹⁴ And I said unto him, Sir, you know. And he said to me, These are they which came out of great tribulation, and have washed their robes, and made them white in the blood of the Lamb. ¹⁵ Therefore are they before the throne of God, and serve him day and night in his

temple: and he that sits on the throne shall dwell among them. ¹⁶ They shall hunger no more, neither thirst any more; neither shall the sun light on them, nor any heat.

¹⁷ For the Lamb which is in the midst of the throne shall feed them, and shall lead them unto living fountains of waters: and God shall wipe away all tears from their eyes.

The Seventh Seal; Seven Angels, Seven Trumpets (Rev 8:1-6)

Chapter 8

And when he had opened the seventh seal, there was silence in heaven about the space of half an hour. ² And I saw the seven angels which stood before God; and to them were given seven trumpets.

³ And another angel came and stood at the altar, having a golden censer; and there was given unto him much incense, that he should offer

it with the prayers of all saints upon the golden altar which was before the throne. **⁴** And the smoke of the incense, which came with the prayers of the saints, ascended up before God out of the angel's hand. **⁵** And the angel took the censer, and filled it with fire of the altar, and cast it into the earth: and there were voices, and thunderings, and lightnings, and an earthquake.

⁶ And the seven angels which had the seven trumpets prepared themselves to sound. **⁷** The first angel sounded, and there followed hail and fire mingled with blood, and they were cast upon the earth: and the third part of trees was burnt up, and all green grass was burnt up. **⁸** And the second angel sounded, and as it were a great mountain burning with fire was cast into the sea: and the third part of the sea became blood; **⁹** And the third part of the creatures which were in the sea, and had life, died; and the third part of the ships were destroyed.

The First Six Trumpet Judgements (Rev 8:7-13 and Rev 9)

¹⁰And the third angel sounded, and there fell a great star from heaven, burning as it were a lamp, and it fell upon the third part of the rivers, and upon the fountains of waters; ¹¹And the name of the star is called Wormwood: and the third part of the waters became Wormwood; and many men died of the waters, because they were made bitter.

¹²And the fourth angel sounded, and the third part of the sun was smitten, and the third part of the moon, and the third part of the stars; so as the third part of them was darkened, and the day shone not for a third part of it, and the night likewise.

¹³And I beheld, and heard an angel flying through the midst of heaven, saying with a loud voice, Woe, woe, woe, to the inhabiters of the earth by reason of the other voices of the trumpet of the three angels, which are yet to sound!

Chapter 9

And the fifth angel sounded, and I saw a star fall from heaven unto the earth: and to him was given the key of the bottomless pit. ²And he opened the bottomless pit; and there arose a smoke out of the pit, as the smoke of a great furnace; and the sun and the air were darkened by reason of the smoke of the pit. ³And there came out of the smoke locusts upon the earth: and unto them was given power, as the scorpions of the earth have power. ⁴And it was commanded them that they should not hurt the grass of the earth, neither any green thing, neither any tree; but only those men which have not the seal of God in their foreheads. ⁵And to them it was given that they should not kill them, but that they should be tormented five months: and their torment was as the torment of a scorpion, when he strikes a man. ⁶And in those days shall men seek death, and shall not find it; and shall desire to die, and death shall flee from them.

⁷And the shapes of the locusts were like unto horses prepared unto battle; and on their heads were as it were crowns like gold, and their faces were as the faces of men. ⁸And they had hair as the hair of women, and their teeth were as the teeth of lions. ⁹And they had breastplates, as it were breastplates of iron; and the sound of their wings was as the sound of chariots of many horses running to battle. ¹⁰And they had tails like unto scorpions, and there were stings in their tails: and their power was to hurt men five months.

¹¹And they had a king over them, which is the angel of the bottomless pit, whose name in the Hebrew tongue is Abaddon, but in the Greek tongue hath his name Apollyon.

¹²One woe is past; and, behold, there come two woes more hereafter.

¹³And the sixth angel sounded, and I heard a voice from the four horns of the golden altar which is before God, ¹⁴Saying to the sixth angel which had the trumpet, Loose the four angels which are bound in the great river Euphrates. ¹⁵And the four angels were loosed, which were prepared for an hour, and a day, and a month, and a year, for to slay the third part of men. ¹⁶And the number of the army of the horsemen were two hundred thousand thousand: and I heard the number of them.

¹⁷And thus I saw the horses in the vision, and them that sat on them, having breastplates of fire, and of jacinth, and brimstone: and the heads of the horses were as the heads of lions; and out of their mouths issued fire and smoke and brimstone. ¹⁸By these three was the third part of men killed, by the fire, and by the smoke, and by the brimstone, which issued out of their mouths. ¹⁹For their power is in their mouth, and in their tails: for their tails were like unto serpents, and had heads, and with them they do hurt.

²⁰And the rest of the men which were not killed by these plagues yet repented not of the works of their hands, that they should not worship devils, and idols of gold, and silver, and brass, and stone, and of wood: which neither can see, nor hear, nor walk: ²¹Neither repented they of their murders, nor of their sorceries, nor of their fornication, nor of their thefts.

Chapter 10

And I saw another mighty angel come down from heaven, clothed with a cloud: and a rainbow was upon his head, and his face was as it were the sun, and his feet as pillars of fire: ²And he had in his hand a little book open: and he set his right foot upon the sea, and his left foot on the earth, ³And cried with a loud voice, as when a lion roars: and when he had cried, seven thunders uttered their voices. ⁴And when the seven thunders had uttered their voices, I was about to write: and I heard a voice from heaven saying unto me, Seal up those things which the seven thunders uttered, and write them not.

The Angel and the Little Scroll (Rev 10)

⁵And the angel which I saw stand upon the sea and upon the earth lifted up his hand to heaven,

⁶ And swear by him that lives for ever and ever, who created heaven, and the things that therein are, and the earth, and the things that therein are, and the sea, and the things which are therein, that there should be time no longer: ⁷ But in the days of the voice of the seventh angel, when he shall begin to sound, the mystery of God should be finished, as he hath declared to his servants the prophets.

⁸ And the voice which I heard from heaven spoke unto me again, and said, Go and take the little book which is open in the hand of the angel which stands upon the sea and upon the earth.

⁹ And I went unto the angel, and said unto him, Give me the little book. And he said unto me, Take it, and eat it up; and it shall make thy belly bitter, but it shall be in thy mouth sweet as honey. ¹⁰ And I took the little book out of the angel's hand, and ate it up; and it was in my mouth sweet as honey: and as soon as I had eaten it, my belly was bitter. ¹¹ And he said unto me, You must prophesy again before many

The Two Witnesses and the Seventh Trumpet Judgement (Rev 11:1-6)

peoples, and nations, and tongues, and kings.

Chapter 11

And there was given me a reed like unto a rod: and the angel stood, saying, Rise, and measure the temple of God, and the altar, and them that worship therein. ² But the court which is without the temple leave out, and measure it not; for it is given unto the Gentiles: and the holy city shall they tread under foot forty and two months. ³ And I will give power unto my two witnesses, and they shall prophesy a thousand two hundred and threescore days, clothed in sackcloth. ⁴ These are the two olive trees, and the two candlesticks standing before the God of the earth. ⁵ And if any man will hurt them, fire proceeds out of their mouth, and devours their enemies: and if any man will hurt them, he must in this manner be killed. ⁶ These have power to shut heaven, that it rain not in the days of their prophecy: and have power over waters to turn them to blood, and to smite the earth with all plagues, as often as they will.

⁷ And when they shall have finished their testimony, the beast that ascends out of the bottomless pit shall make war against them, and shall overcome them, and kill them. ⁸ And their dead bodies shall lie in the street of the great city, which spiritually is called Sodom and Egypt, where also our Lord was crucified. ⁹ And they of the people and kindreds and tongues and nations shall see their dead bodies three days and an half, and shall not suffer their dead bodies to be put in graves.

¹⁰ And they that dwell upon the earth shall rejoice over them, and make merry, and shall send gifts one to another; because these two prophets tormented them that dwelt on the earth.

¹¹ And after three days and an half the spirit of life from God entered into them, and they stood upon their feet; and great fear fell upon them which saw them. ¹² And they heard a great voice from heaven saying unto them, Come up hither. And they ascended up to heaven in a cloud; and their enemies beheld them.

The Two Witnesses Being Taken Up Into Heaven (Rev 11:7-13)

¹³ And the same hour was there a great earthquake, and the tenth part of the city fell, and in the earthquake were slain of men seven thousand: and the remnant were affrighted, and gave glory to the God of heaven.

¹⁴ The second woe is past; and, behold, the third woe comes quickly.

¹⁵ And the seventh angel sounded; and there were great voices in heaven, saying, The kingdoms of this world are become the kingdoms of our Lord, and of his Christ; and he shall reign for ever and ever.

¹⁶ And the four and twenty elders, which sat before God on their seats, fell upon their faces, and worshipped God, ¹⁷ Saying, We give thee thanks, O LORD God Almighty, which art, and was, and art to come; because you have taken to thee thy great power, and have reigned. ¹⁸ And the nations were angry, and thy wrath is come, and the time of the dead, that they should be judged, and that you should give reward unto thy servants the prophets, and to the saints, and them that fear thy name, small and great; and should destroy them which destroy the earth. ¹⁹ And the temple of God was opened in heaven, and there was seen in his temple the ark of his testament: and there were lightning, and voices, and thunder, and an earthquake, and great hail.

Chapter 12

And there appeared a great wonder in heaven; a woman clothed with the sun, and the moon under her feet, and upon her head a crown of twelve stars: ² And she being with child cried, travailing in birth, and pained to be delivered. ³ And there appeared another wonder in heaven; and behold a great red dragon, having seven heads and ten horns, and seven crowns upon his heads. ⁴ And his tail drew the third part of the stars of heaven, and did cast them to the earth: and the dragon stood before the woman which was ready to be delivered, for to devour her child as soon as it was born. ⁵ And she brought forth a man child, who was to rule all nations with a rod of iron: and her child was caught up unto God, and to his throne. ⁶ And the woman fled into the wilderness, where she hath a place prepared of God, that they should feed her there a thousand two hundred and threescore days.

⁷ And there was war in heaven: Michael and his angels fought against the dragon; and the dragon fought and his angels, ⁸ And prevailed not;

The Woman and the Dragon (Rev 12:1-5)

War In Heaven; Michael Defeats the Dragon (Rev 12:7-12)

neither was their place found any more in heaven. ⁹ And the great dragon was cast out, that old serpent, called the Devil, and Satan, which deceives the whole world: he was cast out into the earth, and his angels were cast out with him.

¹⁰And I heard a loud voice saying in heaven, Now is come salvation, and strength, and the kingdom of our God, and the power of his Christ: for the accuser of our brethren is cast down, which accused them before our God day and night.

¹¹And they overcame him by the blood of the Lamb, and by the word of their testimony; and they loved not their lives unto the death.

Woman With the Wings of An Eagle (Rev 12:14)

¹² Therefore rejoice, ye heavens, and ye that dwell in them. Woe to the inhabiters of the earth and of the sea! for the devil is come down unto you, having great wrath, because he knows that he hath but a short time.

¹³ And when the dragon saw that he was cast unto the earth, he persecuted the woman which brought forth the man child. ¹⁴ And to the woman were given two wings of a great eagle, that she might fly into the wilderness, into her place, where she is nourished for a time, and times, and half a time, from the face of the serpent. ¹⁵ And the serpent cast out of his mouth water as a flood after the woman, that he might cause her to be carried away of the flood. ¹⁶ And the earth helped the woman, and the earth opened her mouth, and swallowed up the

The Dragon Spewing Water, Pursues the Woman (Rev 12:15-17)

flood which the dragon cast out of his mouth. ¹⁷ And the dragon was wroth with the woman, and went to make war with the remnant of her seed, which keep the commandments of God, and have the testimony of Jesus Christ.

Chapter 13

And I stood upon the sand of the sea, and saw a beast rise up out of the sea, having seven heads and ten horns, and upon his horns ten crowns, and upon his heads the name of blasphemy. ² And the beast which I saw was like unto a leopard, and his feet were as the feet of a bear, and his mouth as the mouth of a lion: and the dragon gave him his power, and his seat, and great authority. ³ And I saw one of his heads as it were wounded to death; and his deadly wound was healed: and all the world wondered after the beast. ⁴ And they worshipped the dragon which gave power unto the beast: and they worshipped the beast, saying, Who is like unto the beast? Who is able to make war with him?

⁵ And there was given unto him a mouth speaking great things and blasphemies; and power was given unto him to continue forty and two months. ⁶ And he opened his mouth in blasphemy against God, to blaspheme his name, and his tabernacle, and them that dwell in heaven. ⁷ And it was given unto him to make war with the saints, and to overcome them: and power was given him over all kindreds, and tongues, and nations. ⁸ And all that dwell upon the earth shall worship him, whose names are not written in the book of life of the Lamb slain from the foundation of the world.

The Three Beasts and 666 (Rev 13)

⁹ If any man have an ear, let him hear. ¹⁰ He that leads into captivity shall go into captivity: he that kills with the sword must be killed with the sword. Here is the patience and the faith of the saints.

¹¹ And I beheld another beast coming up out of the earth; and he had two horns like a lamb, and he spoke as a dragon. ¹² And he exercises all the power of the first beast before him, and causes the earth and them which dwell therein to worship the first beast, whose deadly wound was healed. ¹³ And he doeth great wonders, so that he maketh fire come down from heaven on the earth in the sight of men, ¹⁴ And deceives them that dwell on the earth by the means of those miracles which he had power to do in the sight of the beast; saying to them that dwell on the earth, that they should make an image to the beast, which had the wound by a sword, and did live. ¹⁵ And he had power to give life unto the image of the beast, that the image of the beast should both speak, and cause that as many as would not worship the image of the beast should be killed. ¹⁶ And he causes all, both small and great, rich and poor, free and bond, to receive a mark in their right hand, or in their foreheads: ¹⁷ And that no man might buy or sell, save he that had the mark, or the name of the beast, or the number of his name.

¹⁸ Here is wisdom. Let him that hath understanding count the number of the beast: for it is the number of a man; and his number is Six hundred threescore and six.

Chapter 14

And I looked, and, lo, a Lamb stood on the mount Zion, and with him an hundred forty and four thousand, having his Father's name written in their foreheads. ² And I heard a voice from heaven, as the voice of many waters, and as the voice of a great thunder: and I heard the voice of harpers harping with their harps: ³ And they sung as it were a new song before the throne, and before the four beasts, and the elders: and no man could learn that song but the hundred and forty and four thousand, which were redeemed from the earth. ⁴ These are they which were not defiled with women; for they are virgins. These are they which follow the Lamb whithersoever he goes. These were redeemed from among men, being the first fruits unto God and to the Lamb. ⁵ And in their mouth was found no guile: for they are without fault before the throne of God.

⁶ And I saw another angel fly in the midst of heaven, having the everlasting gospel to preach unto them that dwell on the earth, and to every nation, and kindred, and tongue, and people, ⁷ Saying with a loud voice, Fear God, and give glory to him; for the hour of his judgment is come: and worship him that made heaven, and earth, and the sea, and the fountains of waters.

⁸ And there followed another angel, saying, Babylon is fallen, is fallen, that great city, because she made all nations drink of the wine of the wrath of her fornication.

⁹ And the third angel followed them, saying with a loud voice, If any man worship the beast and his image, and receive his mark in his forehead, or in his hand, ¹⁰ The same shall drink of the wine of the wrath of God, which is poured out without mixture into the cup of his indignation; and he shall be tormented with fire and brimstone in the presence of the holy angels, and in the presence of the Lamb: ¹¹ And the smoke of their torment ascends up for ever and ever: and they have no rest day nor night, who worship the beast and his image, and whosoever receives the mark of his name. ¹² Here is the patience of the saints: here are they that keep the commandments of God, and the faith of Jesus.

¹³ And I heard a voice from heaven saying unto me, Write, Blessed are the dead which die in the Lord from henceforth: Yea, says the Spirit, that they may rest from their labors; and their works do follow them.

¹⁴ And I looked, and behold a white cloud, and upon the cloud one sat like unto the Son of man, having on his head a golden crown, and in his hand a sharp sickle. ¹⁵ And another angel came out of the temple, crying with a loud voice to him that sat on the cloud, Thrust in thy sickle, and reap: for the time is come for thee to reap; for the harvest of the earth is ripe. ¹⁶ And he that sat on the cloud thrust in his sickle on the earth; and the earth was reaped.

¹⁷ And another angel came out of the temple which is in heaven, he also having a sharp sickle. ¹⁸ And another angel came out from the altar, which had power over fire; and cried with a loud cry to him that had the sharp sickle, saying, Thrust in thy sharp sickle, and gather

the clusters of the vine of the earth; for her grapes are fully ripe. ¹⁹ And the angel thrust in his sickle into the earth, and gathered the vine of the earth, and cast it into the great winepress of the wrath of God. ²⁰ And the winepress was trodden without the city, and blood came out of the winepress, even unto the horse bridles, by the space of a thousand and six hundred furlongs.

The Seven Vial (Bowl) Judgements (Rev 15)

Chapter 15

And I saw another sign in heaven, great and marvelous, seven angels having the seven last plagues; for in them is filled up the wrath of God. ² And I saw as it were a sea of glass mingled with fire: and them that had gotten the victory over the beast, and over his image, and over his mark, and over the number of his name, stand on the sea of glass, having the harps of God. ³ And they sing the song of Moses the servant of God, and the song of the Lamb, saying, Great and marvelous are thy works, Lord God Almighty; just and true are thy ways, you King of saints. ⁴ Who shall not fear thee, O Lord, and glorify thy name? for you only art holy: for all nations shall come and worship before thee; for thy judgments are made manifest.

⁵ And after that I looked, and, behold, the temple of the tabernacle of the testimony in heaven was opened: ⁶ And the seven angels came out of the temple, having the seven plagues, clothed in pure and white linen, and having their breasts girded with golden girdles. ⁷ And one of the four beasts gave unto the seven angels seven golden vials full of the wrath of God, who lives for ever and ever. ⁸ And the temple was filled with smoke from the glory of God, and from his power; and no man was able to enter into the temple, till the seven plagues of the seven angels were fulfilled.

The Plagues of the Seven Vials (Bowls) (Rev 16)

Chapter 16

And I heard a great voice out of the temple saying to the seven angels, Go your ways, and pour out the vials of the wrath of God upon the earth.

² And the first went, and poured out his vial upon the earth; and there fell a noisome and grievous sore upon the men which had the mark of the beast, and upon them which worshipped his image.

³ And the second angel poured out his vial upon the sea; and it became as the blood of a dead man: and every living soul died in the sea.

⁴ And the third angel poured out his vial upon the rivers and fountains of waters; and they became blood. ⁵ And I heard the angel of the waters say, You art righteous, O Lord, which art, and wast, and shalt be, because you have judged thus. ⁶ For they have shed the blood of saints and prophets, and you have given them blood to drink; for they are worthy. ⁷ And I heard another out of the altar say, Even so, Lord God Almighty, true and righteous are thy judgments.

⁸ And the fourth angel poured out his vial upon the sun; and power was given unto him to scorch men with fire. ⁹ And men were scorched with great heat, and blasphemed the name of God, which hath power over these plagues: and they repented not to give him glory.

¹⁰ And the fifth angel poured out his vial upon the seat of the beast; and his kingdom was full of darkness; and they gnawed their tongues for pain, ¹¹ And blasphemed the God of heaven because of their pains and their sores, and repented not of their deeds. ¹² And the sixth angel poured out his vial upon the great river Euphrates; and the water thereof was dried up, that the way of the kings of the east might be prepared. ¹³ And I saw three unclean spirits like frogs come out of the mouth of the dragon, and out of the mouth of the beast, and out of the mouth of the false prophet. ¹⁴ For they are the spirits of devils, working miracles, which go forth unto the kings of the earth and of the whole world, to gather them to the battle of that great day of God Almighty.

¹⁵ Behold, I come as a thief. Blessed is he that watches, and keeps his garments, lest he walk naked, and they see his shame. ¹⁶ And he gathered them together into a place called in the Hebrew tongue Armageddon.

¹⁷ And the seventh angel poured out his vial into the air; and there came a great voice out of the temple of heaven, from the throne, saying, It is done. ¹⁸ And there were voices, and thunder, and lightning; and there was a great earthquake, such as was not since men were upon the earth, so mighty an earthquake, and so great. ¹⁹ And the great city was divided into three parts, and the cities of the nations fell: and great Babylon came in remembrance before God, to give unto her the cup of the wine of the fierceness of his wrath. ²⁰ And every island fled away, and the mountains were not found. ²¹ And there fell upon men a great hail out of heaven, every stone about the weight of a talent: and men blasphemed God because of the plague of the hail; for the plague thereof was exceeding great.

Chapter 17

And there came one of the seven angels which had the seven vials, and talked with me, saying unto me, Come hither; I will show unto thee the judgment of the great whore that sits upon many waters: ² With whom the kings of the earth have committed fornication, and the inhabitants of the earth have been made drunk with the wine of her fornication.

³ So he carried me away in the spirit into the wilderness: and I saw a woman sit upon a scarlet colored beast, full of names of blasphemy, having seven heads and ten horns. ⁴ And the woman was arrayed in purple and scarlet color, and decked with gold and precious stones and pearls, having a golden cup in her hand full of abominations and filthiness of her fornication: ⁵ And upon her forehead was a name written,

**MYSTERY,
BABYLON THE GREAT,
THE MOTHER OF HARLOTS
AND ABOMINATIONS OF THE EARTH.**

⁶ And I saw the woman drunken with the blood of the saints, and with the blood of the martyrs of Jesus: and when I saw her, I wondered with great admiration.

⁷ And the angel said unto me, Wherefore didst you marvel? I will tell thee the mystery of the woman, and of the beast that carrieth her, which hath the seven heads and ten horns. ⁸ The beast that you saw was, and is not; and shall ascend out of the bottomless pit, and go into perdition: and they that dwell on the earth shall wonder, whose names were not written in the book of life from the foundation of the world, when they behold the beast that was, and is not, and yet is.

⁹ And here is the mind which hath wisdom. The seven heads are seven mountains, on which the woman sits. ¹⁰ And there are seven kings: five are fallen, and one is, and the other is not yet come; and when he comes, he must continue a short space. ¹¹ And the beast that was, and is not, even he is the eighth, and is of the seven, and goes into perdition.

¹² And the ten horns which you saw are ten kings, which have received no kingdom as yet; but receive power as kings one hour with the beast.

¹³ These have one mind, and shall give their power and strength unto the beast. ¹⁴ These shall make war with the Lamb, and the Lamb shall overcome them: for he is Lord of lords, and King of kings: and they that are with him are called, and chosen, and faithful.

¹⁵ And he saith unto me, The waters which you saw, where the whore sits, are peoples, and multitudes, and nations, and tongues. ¹⁶ And the ten horns which you saw upon the beast, these shall hate the whore, and shall make her desolate and naked, and shall eat her flesh, and burn her with fire. ¹⁷ For God hath put in their hearts to fulfil his will, and to agree, and give their kingdom unto the beast, until the words of God shall be fulfilled. ¹⁸ And the woman which you saw is that great city, which reigns over the kings of the earth.

Babylon the Great Riding the Beast (Rev 17)

Chapter 18

And after these things I saw another angel come down from heaven, having great power; and the earth was lightened with his glory. ² And he cried mightily with a strong voice, saying, Babylon the great is fallen, is fallen, and is become the habitation of devils, and the hold of every foul spirit, and a cage of every unclean and hateful bird. ³ For all nations have drunk of the wine of the wrath of her fornication, and the kings of the earth have committed fornication with her, and the merchants of the earth are waxed rich through the abundance of her delicacies.

⁴ And I heard another voice from heaven, saying, Come out of her, my people, that ye be not partakers of her sins, and that ye receive not of her plagues. ⁵ For her sins have reached unto heaven, and God hath remembered her iniquities. ⁶ Reward her even as she rewarded you, and double unto her double according to her works: in the cup which she hath filled fill to her double. ⁷ How much she hath glorified herself, and lived deliciously, so much torment and sorrow give her: for she says in her heart, I sit a queen, and am no widow, and shall see no sorrow. ⁸ Therefore shall her plagues come in one day, death, and mourning, and famine; and she shall be utterly burned with fire: for strong is the Lord God who judgeth her.

⁹ And the kings of the earth, who have committed fornication and lived deliciously with her, shall bewail her, and lament for her, when they shall see the smoke of her burning, ¹⁰ Standing afar off for the fear of her torment, saying, Alas, alas that great city Babylon, that mighty city! for in one hour is thy judgment come.

¹¹ And the merchants of the earth shall weep and mourn over her; for no man buyeth their merchandise any more: ¹² The merchandise of gold, and silver, and precious stones, and of pearls, and fine linen, and purple, and silk, and scarlet, and all thyine wood, and all manner vessels of ivory, and all manner vessels of most precious wood, and of brass, and iron, and marble, ¹³ And cinnamon, and odors, and ointments, and frankincense, and wine, and oil, and fine flour, and wheat, and beasts, and sheep, and horses, and chariots, and slaves, and souls of men.

¹⁴ And the fruits that thy soul lusted after are departed from thee, and all things which were dainty and goodly are departed from thee, and you shalt find them no more at all. ¹⁵ The merchants of these things, which were made rich by her, shall stand afar off for the fear of her torment, weeping and wailing, ¹⁶ And saying, Alas, alas that great city, that was clothed in fine linen, and purple, and scarlet, and decked with gold, and precious stones, and pearls!

¹⁷ For in one hour so great riches is come to naught. And every shipmaster, and all the company in ships, and sailors, and as many as trade by sea, stood afar off, ¹⁸ And cried when they saw the smoke of her burning, saying, What city is like unto this great city! ¹⁹ And they cast dust on their heads, and cried, weeping and wailing, saying, Alas, alas that great city, wherein were made rich all that had ships in the sea by reason of her costliness! for in one hour is she made desolate. ²⁰ Rejoice over her, you heaven, and ye holy apostles and prophets; for God hath avenged you on her.

²¹ And a mighty angel took up a stone like a great millstone, and cast it into the sea, saying, Thus with violence shall that great city Babylon be thrown down, and shall be found no more at all. ²² And the voice of harpers, and musicians, and of pipers, and trumpeters, shall be heard no more at all in thee; and no craftsman, of whatsoever craft he be, shall be found any more in thee; and the sound of a millstone shall be heard no more at all in thee; ²³ And the light of a candle shall shine no more at all in thee; and the voice of the bridegroom and of the bride shall be heard no more at all in thee: for thy merchants were the great men of the earth; for by thy sorceries were all nations deceived. ²⁴ And in her was found the blood of prophets, and of saints, and of all that were slain upon the earth.

Chapter 19

And after these things I heard a great voice of much people in heaven, saying, Alleluia; Salvation, and glory, and honor, and power, unto the Lord our God: ² For true and righteous are his judgments: for he hath judged the great whore, which did corrupt the earth with her fornication, and hath avenged the blood of his servants at her hand. ³ And again they said, Alleluia. And her smoke rose up for ever

Angel With Millstone (Rev 18)

and ever.

⁴ And the four and twenty elders and the four beasts fell down and worshipped God that sat on the throne, saying, Amen; Alleluia.

⁵ And a voice came out of the throne, saying, Praise our God, all ye his servants, and ye that fear him, both small and great.

⁶ And I heard as it were the voice of a great multitude, and as the voice of many waters, and as the voice of mighty thunder, saying, Alleluia: for the Lord God omnipotent reigns.

⁷ Let us be glad and rejoice, and give honor to him: for the marriage of the Lamb is come, and his wife hath made herself ready. ⁸ And to her was granted that she should be arrayed in fine linen, clean and white: for the fine linen is the righteousness of saints.

⁹ And he said unto me, Write, Blessed are they which are called unto the marriage supper of the Lamb. And he saith unto me, These are the true sayings of God.

¹⁰ And I fell at his feet to worship him. And he said unto me, See thou do it not: I am thy fellow servant, and of thy brethren that have the testimony of Jesus: worship God: for the testimony of Jesus is the spirit of prophecy.

¹¹ And I saw heaven opened, and behold a white horse; and he that sat upon him was called Faithful and True, and in righteousness he doth judge and make war. ¹² His eyes were as a flame of fire, and on his head were many crowns; and he had

King of kings and Lord of lords (Rev 19:11-16)

a name written, that no man knew, but he himself. ¹³ And he was clothed with a vesture dipped in blood: and his name is called The Word of God. ¹⁴ And the armies which were in heaven followed him upon white horses, clothed in fine linen, white and clean. ¹⁵ And out of his mouth goeth a sharp sword, that with it he should smite the nations: and he shall rule them with a rod of iron: and he treads the winepress of the fierceness and wrath of Almighty God. ¹⁶ And he hath on his vesture and on his thigh a name written,

KING OF KINGS, AND LORD OF LORDS.

¹⁷ And I saw an angel standing in the sun; and he cried with a loud voice, saying to all the fowls that fly in the midst of heaven, Come and gather yourselves together unto the supper of the great God; ¹⁸ That ye may eat the flesh of kings, and the flesh of captains, and the flesh of mighty men, and the flesh of horses, and of them that sit on them, and the flesh of all men, both free and bond, both small and great.

¹⁹ And I saw the beast, and the kings of the earth, and their armies, gathered together to make war against him that sat on the horse, and against his army. ²⁰ And the beast was taken, and with him the false prophet that wrought miracles before him, with which he deceived them that had received the mark of the beast, and them that worshipped his image. These both were cast alive into a lake of fire burning with brimstone. ²¹ And

Beast and the False Prophet Cast Into the Lake of Fire (Rev 19:20)

The Angel With the Great Chain (Rev 20:1-2)

the remnant were slain with the sword of him that sat upon the horse, which sword proceeded out of his mouth: and all the fowls were filled with their flesh.

Chapter 20

And I saw an angel come down from heaven, having the key of the bottomless pit and a great chain in his hand. ² And he laid hold on the dragon, that old serpent, which is the Devil, and Satan, and bound him a thousand years, ³ And cast him into the bottomless pit, and shut him up, and set a seal upon him, that he should deceive the nations no more, till the thousand years should be fulfilled: and after that he must be loosed a little season.

⁴ And I saw thrones, and they sat upon them, and judgment was given unto them: and I saw the souls of them that were beheaded for the witness of Jesus, and for the word of God, and which had not worshipped the beast, neither his image, neither had received his mark upon their foreheads, or in their hands; and they lived and reigned with Christ a thousand years. ⁵ But the rest of the dead lived not again until the thousand years were finished. This is the first resurrection. ⁶ Blessed and holy is he that hath part in the first resurrection: on such the second death hath no power, but they shall be priests of God and of Christ, and shall reign with him a thousand years.

⁷ And when the thousand years are expired, Satan shall be loosed out of his prison, ⁸ And shall go out to deceive the nations which are in the four quarters of the earth, Gog, and Magog, to gather them together to battle: the number of

The Dragon Chained (Rev 20:3)

The Dragon Released To Gather the Nations For Battle (Rev 20:7-8)

whom is as the sand of the sea. ⁹ And they went up on the breadth of the earth, and compassed the camp of the saints about, and the beloved city: and fire came down from God out of heaven, and devoured them. ¹⁰ And the devil that deceived them was cast into the lake of fire and brim where the beast and the false prophet are, and shall be tormented day and night for ever and ever.

¹¹ And I saw a great white throne, and him that sat on it, from whose face the earth and the heaven fled away; and there was found no place for them. ¹² And I saw the dead, small and great, stand before God; and the books were opened: and another book was opened, which is the book of life: and the dead were judged out of those things which were written in the books, according to their works. ¹³ And

The Dragon Thrown Into the Lake of Fire (Rev 20:10)

The Great White Throne Judgement (Rev 20:11-13)

The Books Are Opened and Also the Book of Life (Rev 20:12-13)

the sea gave up the dead which were in it; and death and hell delivered up the dead which were in them: and they were judged every man according to their works. ¹⁴ And death and hell were cast into the lake of fire. This is the second death. ¹⁵ And whosoever was not found written in the book of life was cast into the lake of fire.

The Lake of Fire (Rev 20:14-15)

Chapter 21

And I saw a new heaven and a new earth: for the first heaven and the first earth were passed away; and there was no more sea. ² And I John saw the holy city, new Jerusalem, coming down from God out of heaven, prepared as a bride adorned for her husband. ³ And I heard a great voice out of heaven saying, Behold, the tabernacle of God is with men, and he will dwell with them, and they shall be his people, and God himself shall be with them, and be their God. ⁴ And God shall wipe away all tears from their eyes; and there shall be no more death, neither sorrow, nor crying, neither shall there be any more pain: for the former things are passed away.

⁵ And he that sat upon the throne said, Behold, I make all things new. And he said unto me, Write: for these words are true and faithful.

The City Four-Square; New Jerusalem (Rev 21:1-21)

⁶ And he said unto me, It is done. I am Alpha and Omega, the beginning and the end. I will give unto him that is athirst of the fountain of the water of life freely. ⁷ He that overcometh shall inherit all things; and I will be his God, and he shall be my son. ⁸ But the fearful, and unbelieving, and the abominable, and murderers, and whoremongers, and sorcerers, and idolaters, and all liars, shall have their part in the lake which burns with fire and brimstone: which is the second death.

⁹ And there came unto me one of the seven angels which had the seven vials full of the seven last plagues, and talked with me, saying, Come hither, I will show thee the bride, the Lamb's wife. ¹⁰ And he carried me away in the spirit to a great and high mountain, and showed

The Angel With the Golden Reed (Rod) (Rev 21:15)

me that great city, the holy Jerusalem, descending out of heaven from God, ¹¹ Having the glory of God: and her light was like unto a stone most precious, even like a jasper stone, clear as crystal; ¹² And had a wall great and high, and had twelve gates, and at the gates twelve angels, and names written thereon, which are the names of the twelve tribes of the children of Israel: ¹³ On the east three gates; on the north three gates; on the south three gates; and on the west three gates. ¹⁴ And the wall of the city had twelve foundations, and in them the names of the twelve apostles of the Lamb.¹⁵ And he that talked with me had a golden reed to measure the city, and the gates thereof, and the wall thereof. ¹⁶ And the city lieth foursquare, and the length is as large as the breadth: and he measured the city with the reed, twelve thousand furlongs. The length and the breadth and the height of it are equal. ¹⁷ And he measured the wall thereof, a hundred and forty and four cubits, according to the measure of a man, that is, of the angel. ¹⁸ And the building of the wall of it was of jasper: and the city was pure gold, like unto clear glass. ¹⁹ And the foundations of the wall of the city were garnished with all manner of precious stones. The first foundation was jasper; the second, sapphire; the third, a chalcedony; the fourth, an emerald; ²⁰The fifth, sardonyx; the sixth, sardius; the seventh, chrysolite; the eighth, beryl; the ninth, a topaz; the tenth, a chrysoprasus; the eleventh, a jacinth; the twelfth, an amethyst. ²¹ And the twelve gates were twelve pearls: every several gate was of one pearl: and the street of the city was pure gold, as it were transparent glass.

²² And I saw no temple therein: for the Lord God Almighty and the Lamb are the temple of it. ²³ And the city had no need of the sun, neither of the moon, to shine in it: for the glory of God did lighten it, and the Lamb is the light thereof. ²⁴ And the nations of them which are

The Foundations of the City (Rev 21:12-14 and Rev 21:19-20)

saved shall walk in the light of it: and the kings of the earth do bring their glory and honor into it. [25] And the gates of it shall not be shut at all by day: for there shall be no night there. [26] And they shall bring the glory and honor of the nations into it. [27] And there shall in no wise enter into it any thing that defiles, neither whatsoever works abomination, or makes a lie: but they which are written in the Lamb's book of life.

Chapter 22

And he showed me a pure river of water of life, clear as crystal, proceeding out of the throne of God and of the Lamb. [2] In the midst of the street of it, and on either side of the river, was there the tree of life, which bare twelve manner of fruits, and yielded her fruit every month: and the leaves of the tree were for the healing of the nations. [3] And there shall be no more curse: but the throne of God and of the Lamb shall be in it; and his servants shall serve him: [4] And they shall see his face; and his name shall be in their foreheads. [5] And there shall be no night there; and they need no candle, neither light of the sun; for the Lord God giveth them light: and they shall reign for ever and ever.

[6] And he said unto me, These sayings are faithful and true: and the Lord God of the holy prophets sent his angel to show unto his servants the things which must shortly be done.

[7] Behold, I come quickly: blessed is he that keepeth the sayings of the prophecy of this book.

[8] And I John saw these things, and heard them. And when I had heard and seen, I fell down to worship before the feet of the angel which showed me these things. [9] Then says he unto me, See thou do it not: for I am thy fellow servant, and of thy brethren the prophets, and of them which keep the sayings of this book: worship God.

[10] And he saith unto me, Seal not the sayings of the prophecy of this book: for the time is at hand. [11] He that is unjust, let him be unjust still: and he which is filthy, let him be filthy still: and he that is righteous, let him be righteous still: and he that is holy, let him be holy still.

[12] And, behold, I come quickly; and my reward is with me, to give every man according as his work shall be. [13] I am Alpha and Omega, the beginning and the end, the first and the last.

[14] Blessed are they that do his commandments, that they may have right to the tree of life, and may enter in through the gates into the city. [15] For without are dogs, and sorcerers, and whoremongers, and murderers, and idolaters, and whosoever loveth and maketh a lie.

[16] I Jesus have sent mine angel to testify unto you these things in the churches. I am the root and the offspring of David, and the bright and morning star.

[17] And the Spirit and the bride say, Come. And let him that heareth say, Come. And let him that is thirsty come. And whosoever will, let him take the water of life freely.

[18] For I testify unto every man that heareth the words of the prophecy of this book, If any man shall add unto these things, God shall add unto him the plagues that are written in this book: [19] And if any man shall take away from the words of the book of this prophecy, God shall take away his part out of the book of life, and out of the holy city, and from the things which are written in this book.

[20] He which testifieth these things saith, Surely I come quickly: Amen. Even so, come, Lord Jesus.

[21] The grace of our Lord Jesus Christ be with you all. Amen.

Through the Gate of the Eternal City (Rev 21:21-27 and Rev 22:1-6)

The Rapture

Although it is not specifically described in the text from the Book of Revelation I have decided to include this illustration titled "The Rapture" in this book because I thought it would be a wonderful way to conclude this gallery of prophetic art. ABC News Productions in New York City commissioned me to do this particular illustration in 2005 for a television special they did about what has been known as the Rapture when talking about the return of Christ the Messiah. It was a concept I had been thinking of doing for a while, but had been putting it off. This commission got me motivated to get it done within only two weeks for the program. I prayed for inspiration as I read the scriptures that pertain to this event known as "The Rapture". I thank God for His guidance to create the artwork that resulted.

Rapture is a word that is not actually found in the Bible at all, but it means "a gathering up" and so it is used by Christians to refer to the time when Jesus will gather all His believers up to Himself when He returns. In this illustration, I tried to visualize this great event that is mentioned in various parts of the Bible, the most familiar of which are in Matthew 24 and I Thessalonians 4. Starting on the left bottom of the picture, notice the graves bursting open and the dead who were believers in Christ rising from them, much to the surprise and horror of a passing gardener or grave digger. Moving across the bottom to the center of the picture we see the morning city commute disrupted by driverless vehicles as drivers are "raptured" and taken up. In the foreground a believer and her child are taken up as the unbelieving husband is left behind. And in the lower right corner we see two farmers in a field. One is being taken while the other is left, as Jesus mentions in Matthew 24:40, "*Then shall two be in the field; the one shall be taken, and the other left*". All the raptured believers, dead and alive rise up through the clouds to meet Jesus. I show them growing smaller and smaller as they go up to the top of the painting until they all diverge to become pure white sparkling stars in the gown of the bride. She is the one whom the scriptures symbolically refer to as "the bride of Christ", or in other words, all people who make up Christ's church everywhere. There Jesus waits for her with outstretched arms and a smile on His face. In the background you can see the table that is set for the wedding supper of the Lamb, Jesus.

1 Thessalonians 4:16-18: [16] *For the Lord himself shall descend from heaven with a shout, with the voice of the archangel, and with the trump of God: and the dead in Christ shall rise first:* [17] *Then we which are alive and remain shall be caught up together with them in the clouds, to meet the Lord in the air: and so shall we ever be with the Lord.* [18] *Wherefore comfort one another with these words.*

Although we are not exactly sure of how it will look or when it will occur, we do know that according to all prophetic scripture that it most certainly will happen. We are told in many different scriptures to always be ready for Jesus to return at any moment, day or night. The way to be ready is to believe in and accept Jesus as your Savior, and ask Him to forgive all your sins. Upon being baptized you will receive the gift of the Holy Spirit who will guide you to live as a child of God (Acts 2:38) (Romans 8:13-14). Find a church to attend for regular worship and fellowship together with other believers (Hebrews 10:25). Most importantly, develop a daily personal relationship with God who loves you dearly, by reading His word the Bible, and by keeping in touch with Him every day through prayer. Then you can be sure that your name is written in the Lamb's book of life, and you can look forward to living forever in the glorious new heavens and the new earth!

RESOURCES

Most of the artwork in this book can be ordered as visual teaching materials or art prints from www.revelationillustrated.com

Materials available:

"Revelation Illustrated" **DVD**. This video takes the viewer through Revelation with dramatic narration, classical music and all the Revelation art with added animations and special effects. Just under one hour.
Closed captioned, English and Spanish narration - **$24.95** each.
Discount for 3 or more DVDs ordered at the same time - **$20.00** each, plus shipping*

The *"Revelation Illustrated"* 40 image CD for use in Powerpoint for teaching - **$45.00** each, plus shipping*
(Please note, this CD contains only the art from Revelation, not the Rapture art)

PRINT SET - 35 of the Revelation illustrations are available in 11x14" color prints with scripture reference in border - **$70.00**

16x20" ART PRINTS of "The Emerald Throne Scene in Heaven", "The Opening of the Sealed Scroll", "The Four Horsemen", "War In Heaven", "King of Kings and Lord of Lords", Angel About to Chain the Dragon", "Through the Gate". - **$10.00** each

16x20" Art print of "The Rapture" - **$10.00** plus shipping*

NOTECARDS with scripture on the back and blank inside for your message, includes envelopes. - **$1.00** each, plus shipping*
Titles available are: "The Emerald Throne Scene in Heaven", "The Opening of the Sealed Scroll", "War In Heaven", "King of Kings and Lord of Lords", Angel About to Chain the Dragon", "Through the Gate" and "The Rapture".

Go to our website to see complete details of all our materials and place your order there:
www.revelationillustrated.com
All major charge or debit cards accepted.

Or call 1-800-327-7330 to place your order by phone
*Please call for shipping charges if you decide to order with a check. Ask for our free brochure / catalog.

Revelation Productions
1740 Ridgeview Drive
North Huntingdon, PA 15642 USA
Email: revill@aol.com

Milton Keynes UK
Ingram Content Group UK Ltd.
UKHW051411180823
427107UK00002B/22